I dedicate this book to my husband Scott. Who gave me the idea and confidence to make my love of art and the creativity of Zentangling Fun come true.

This book belongs to:

Colored by:

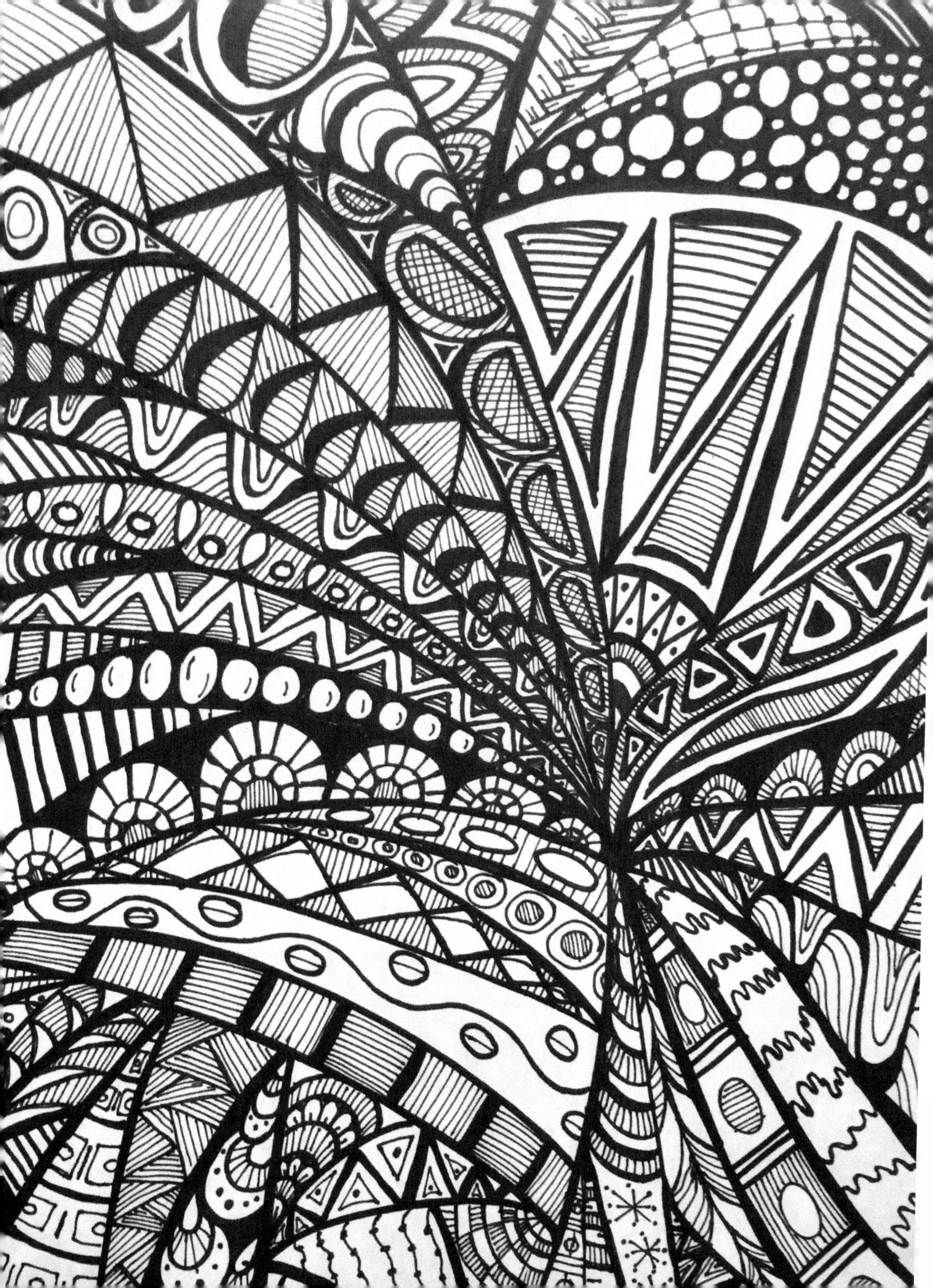

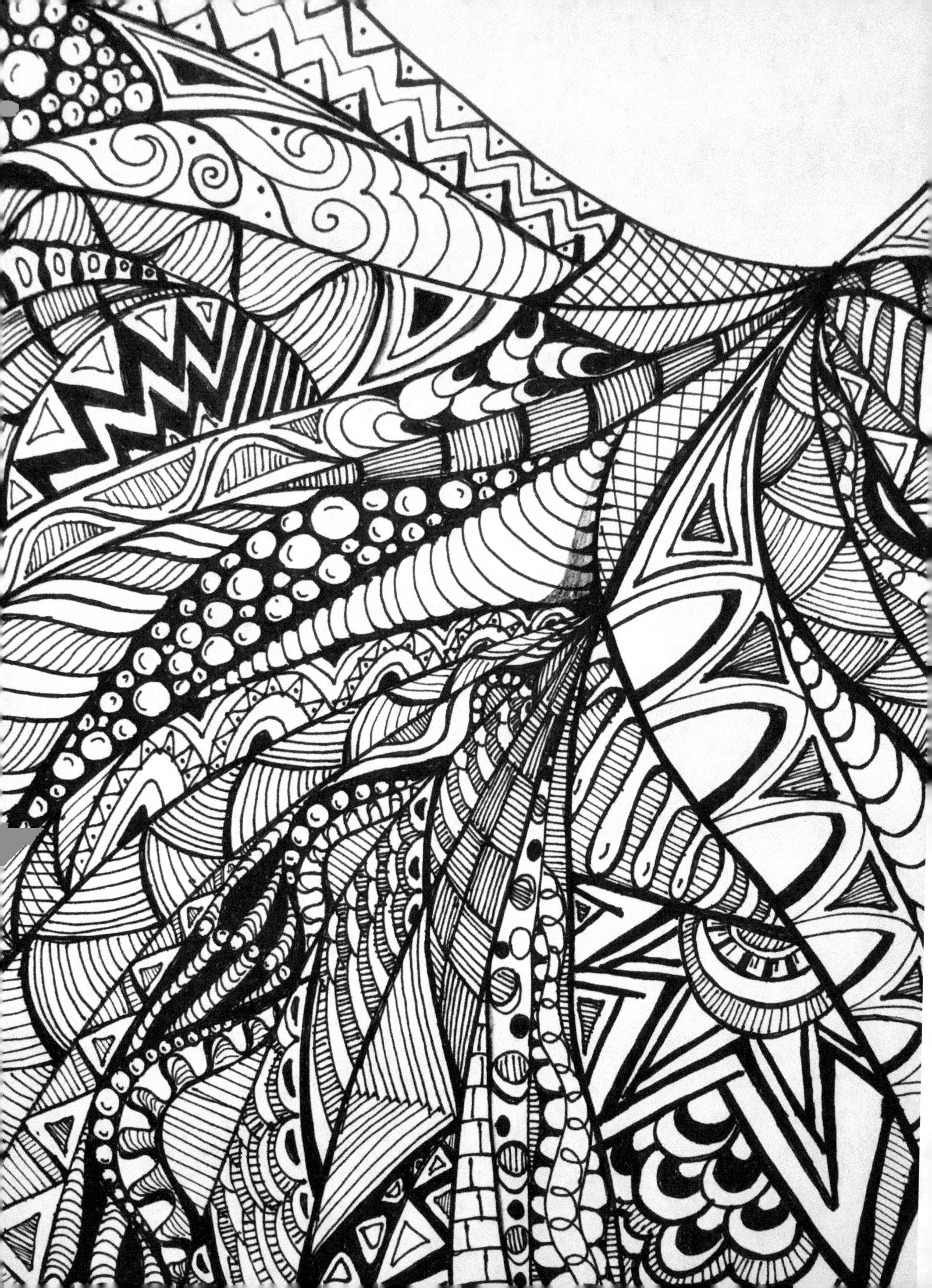

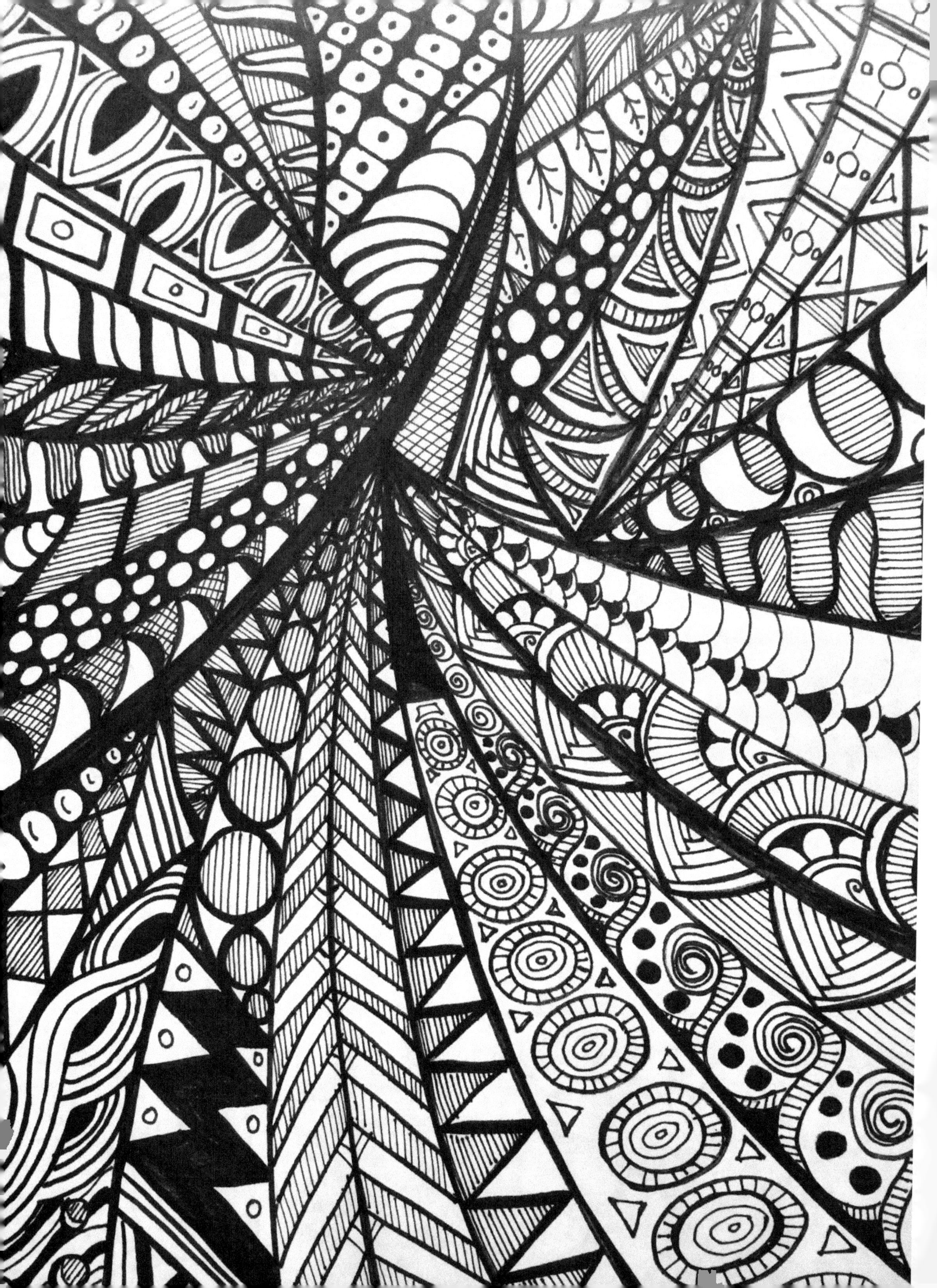

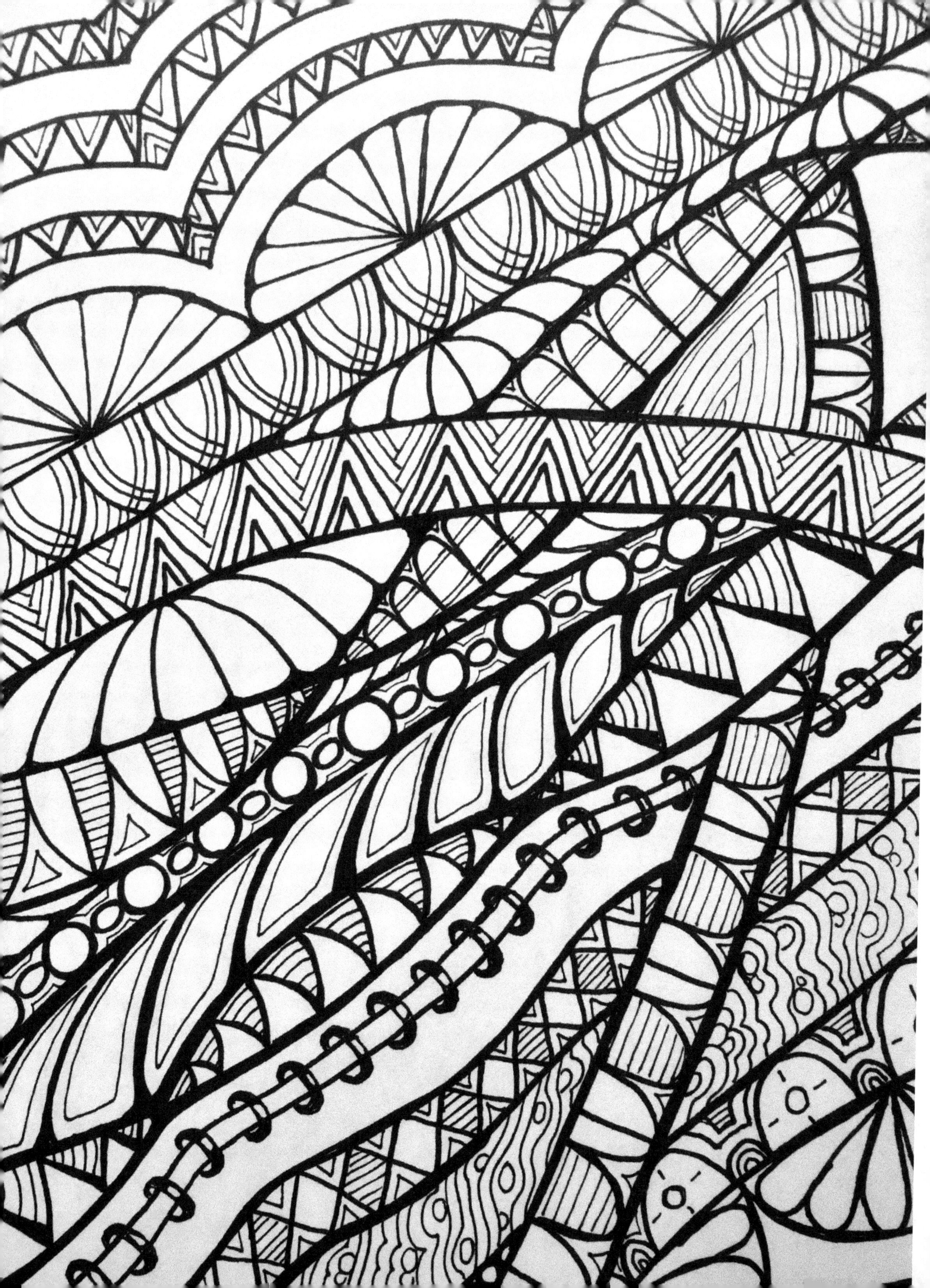

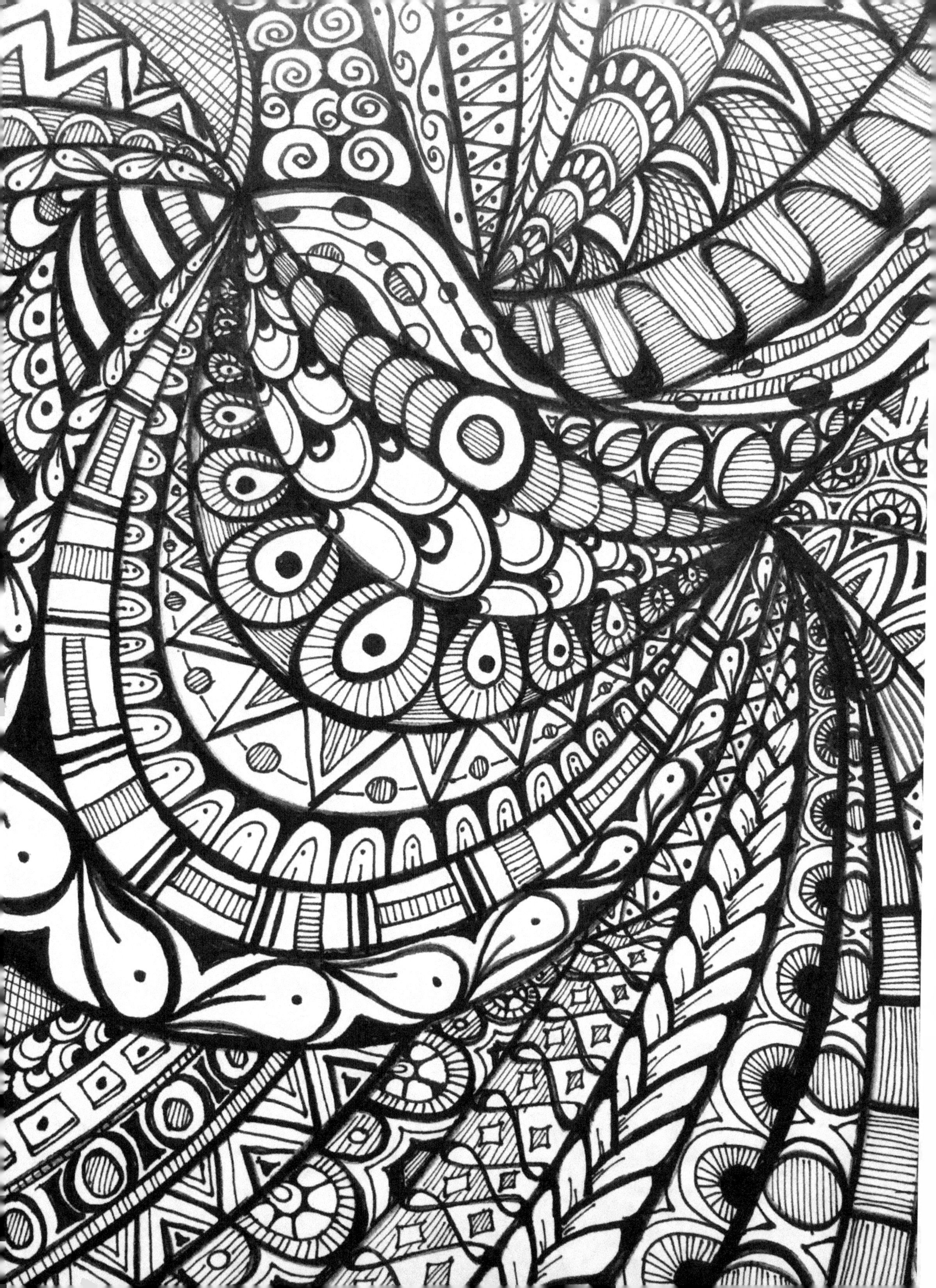

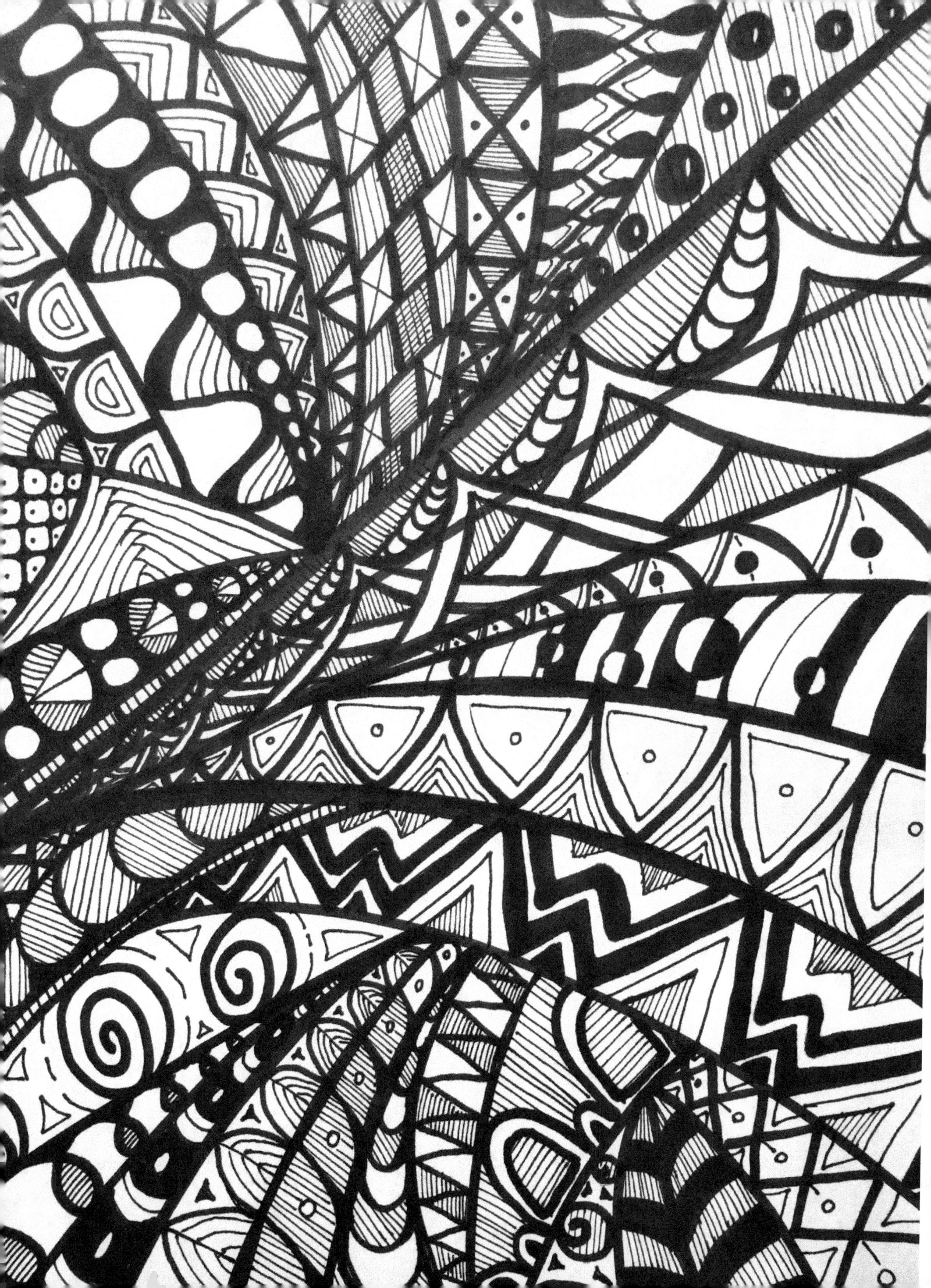

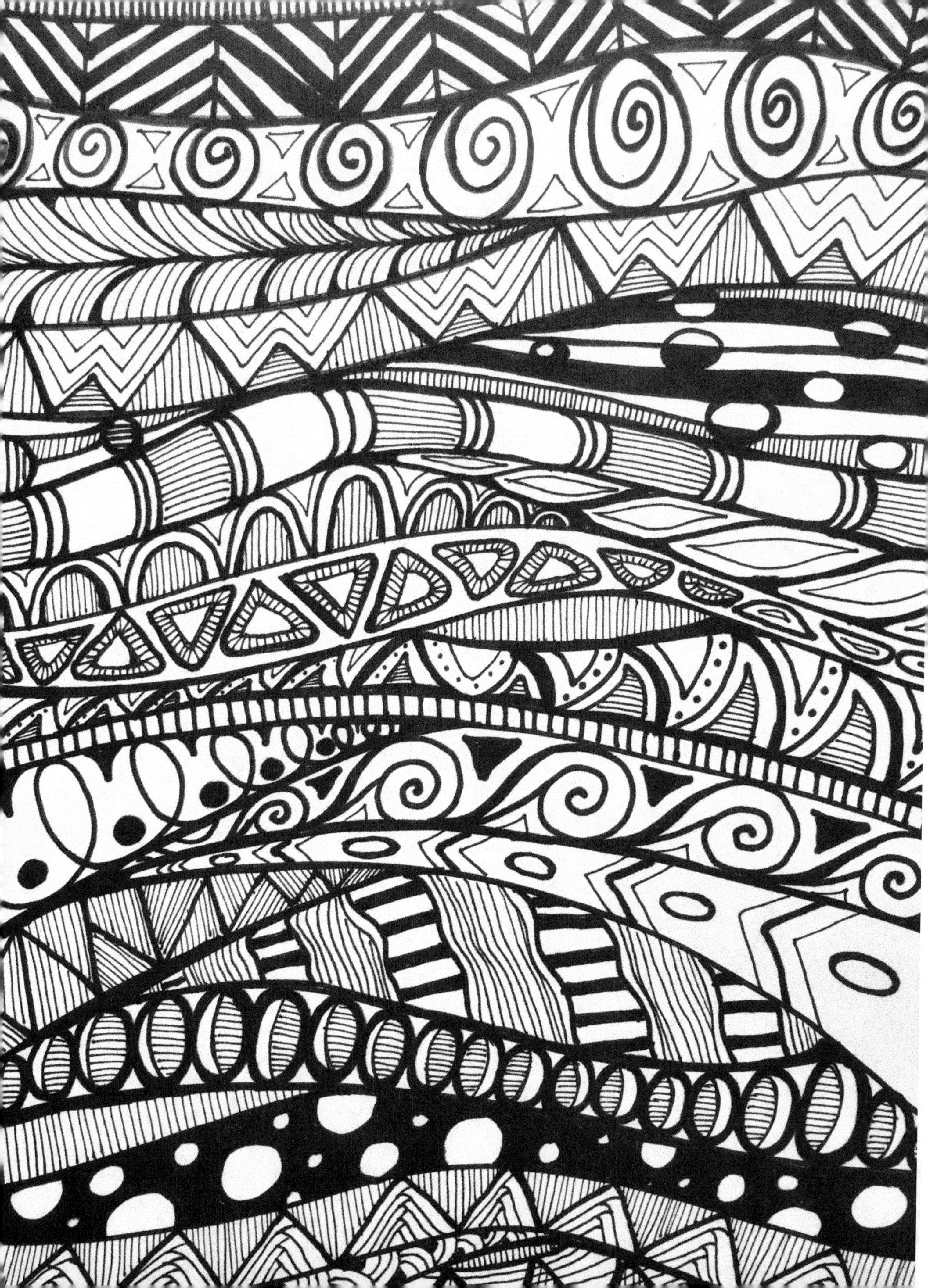

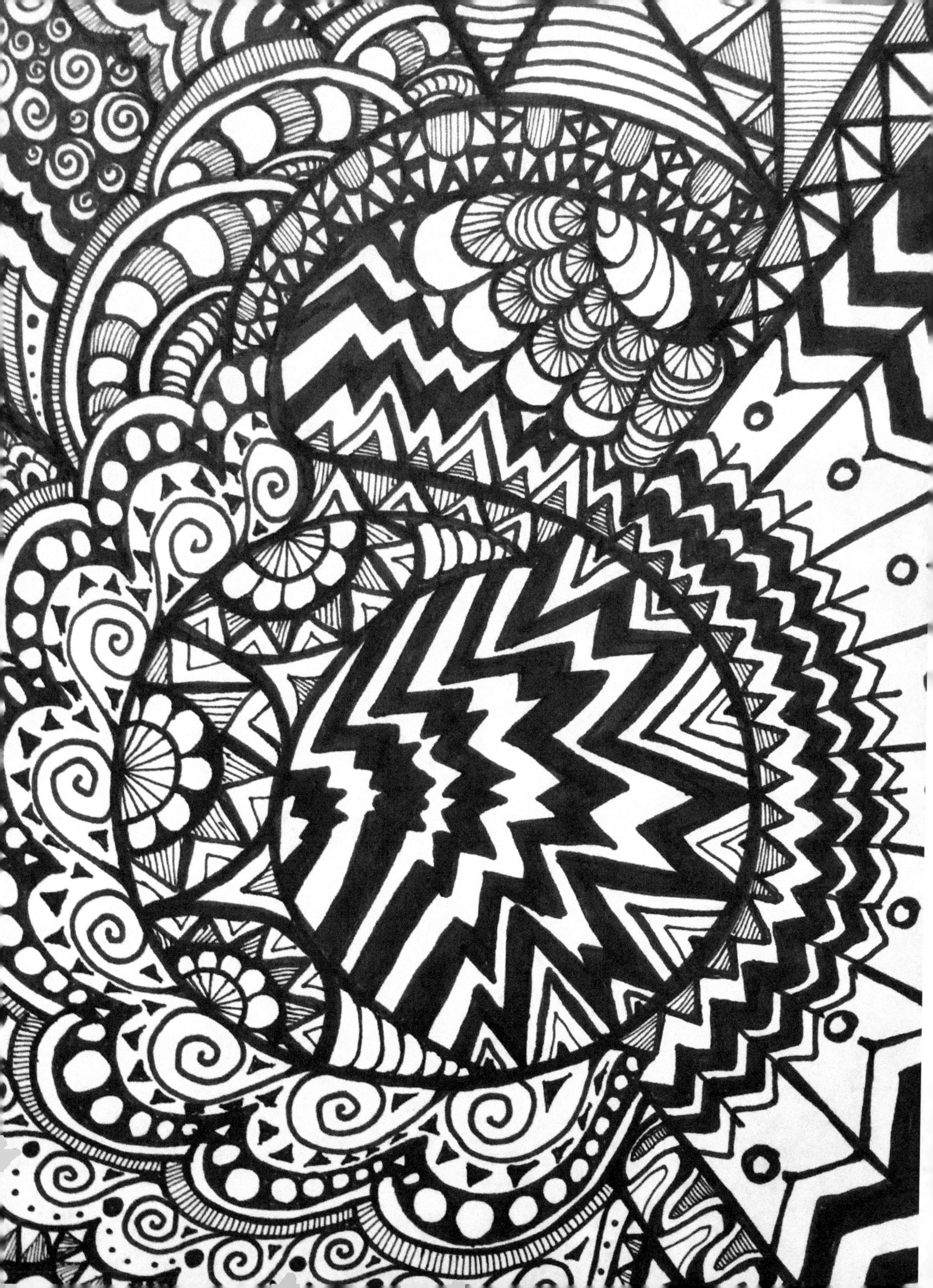

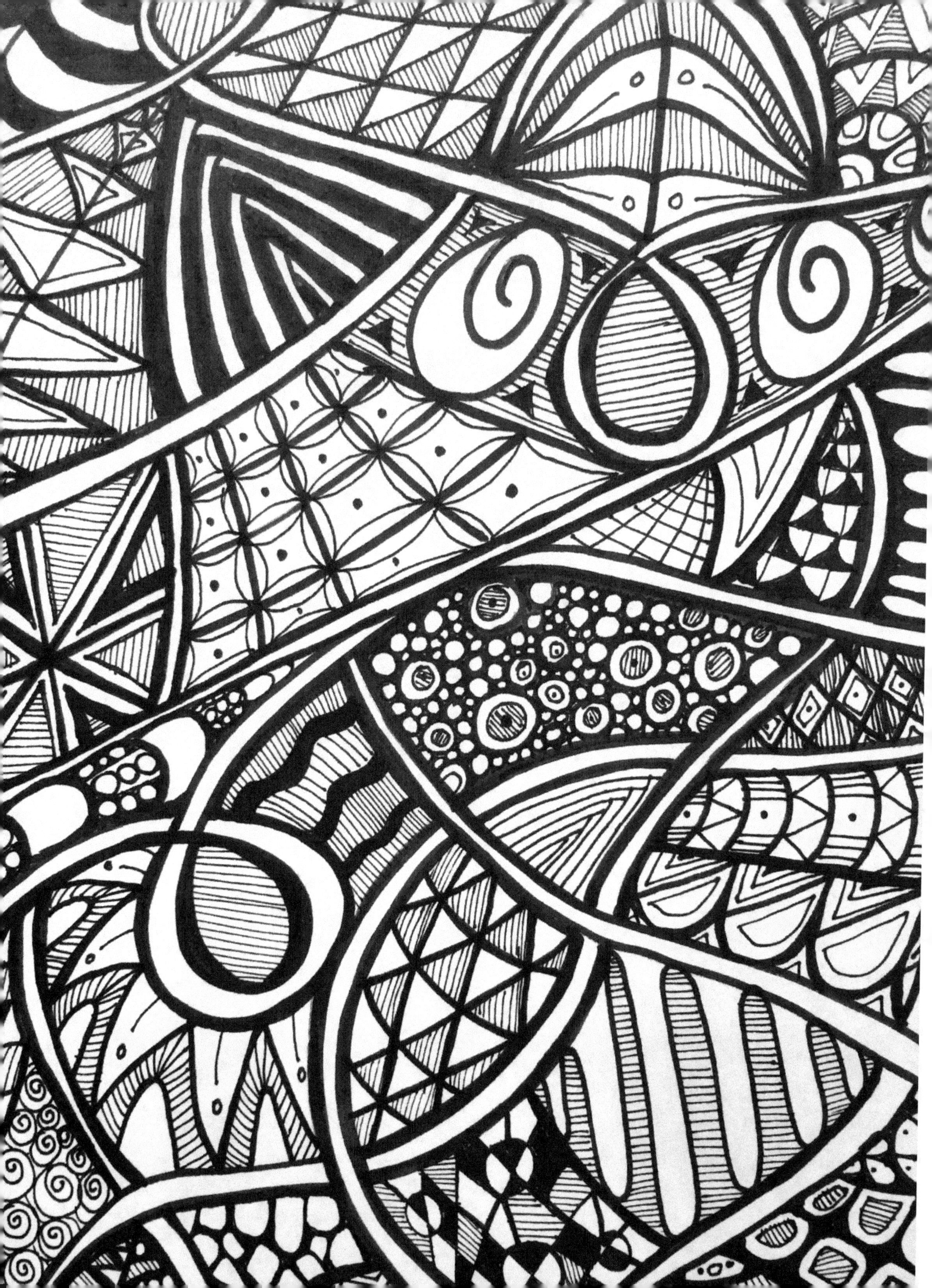

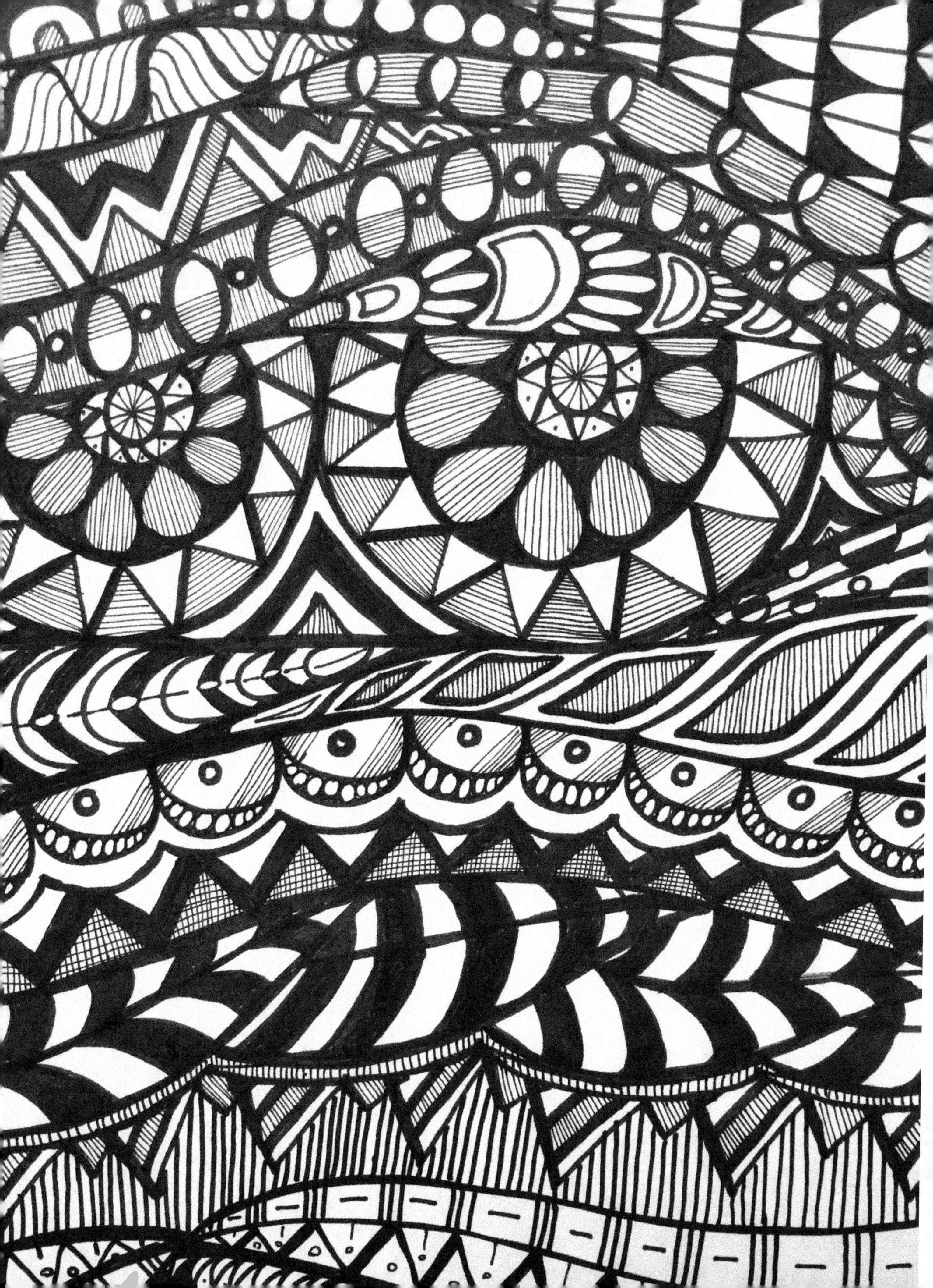

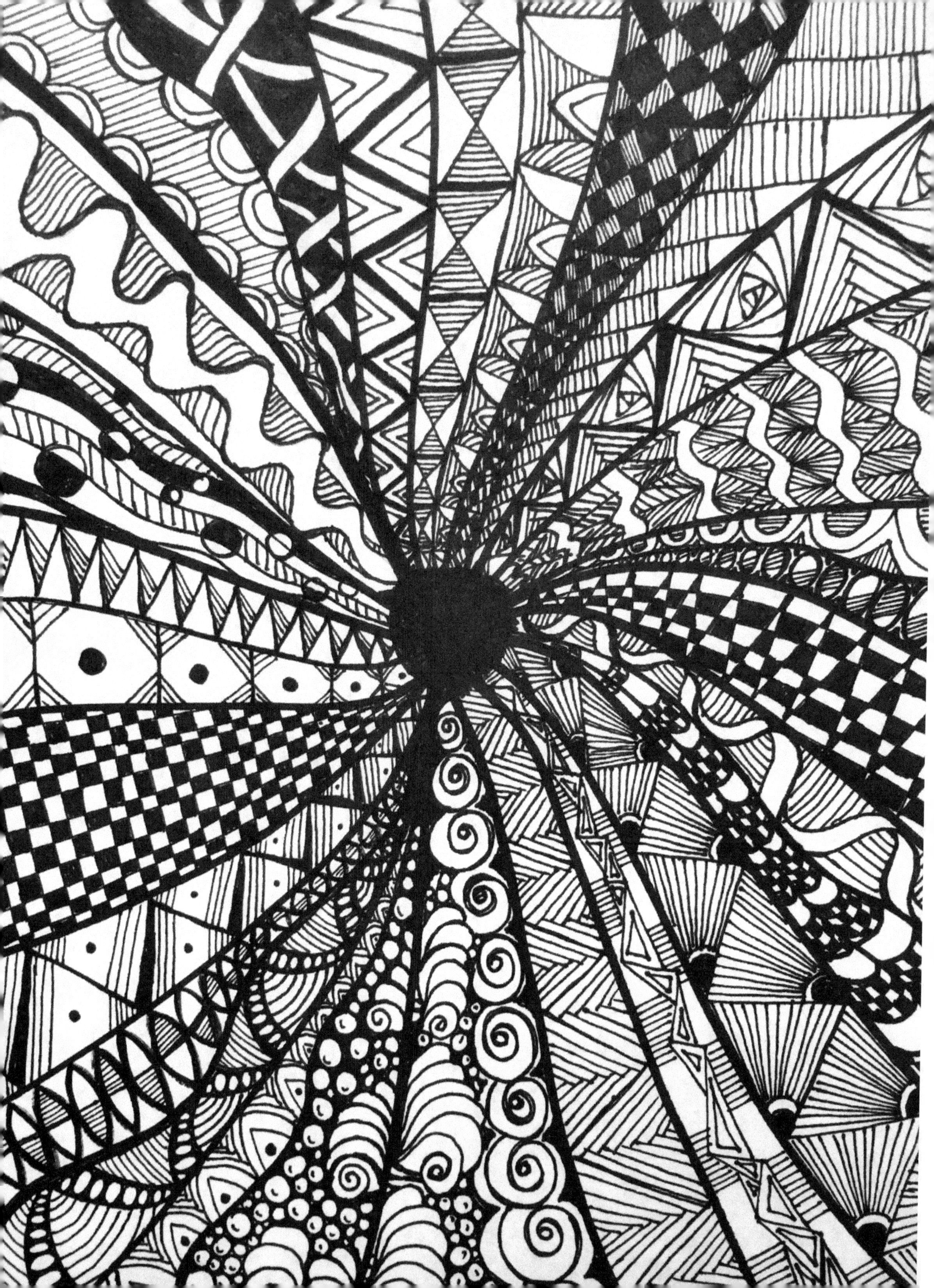

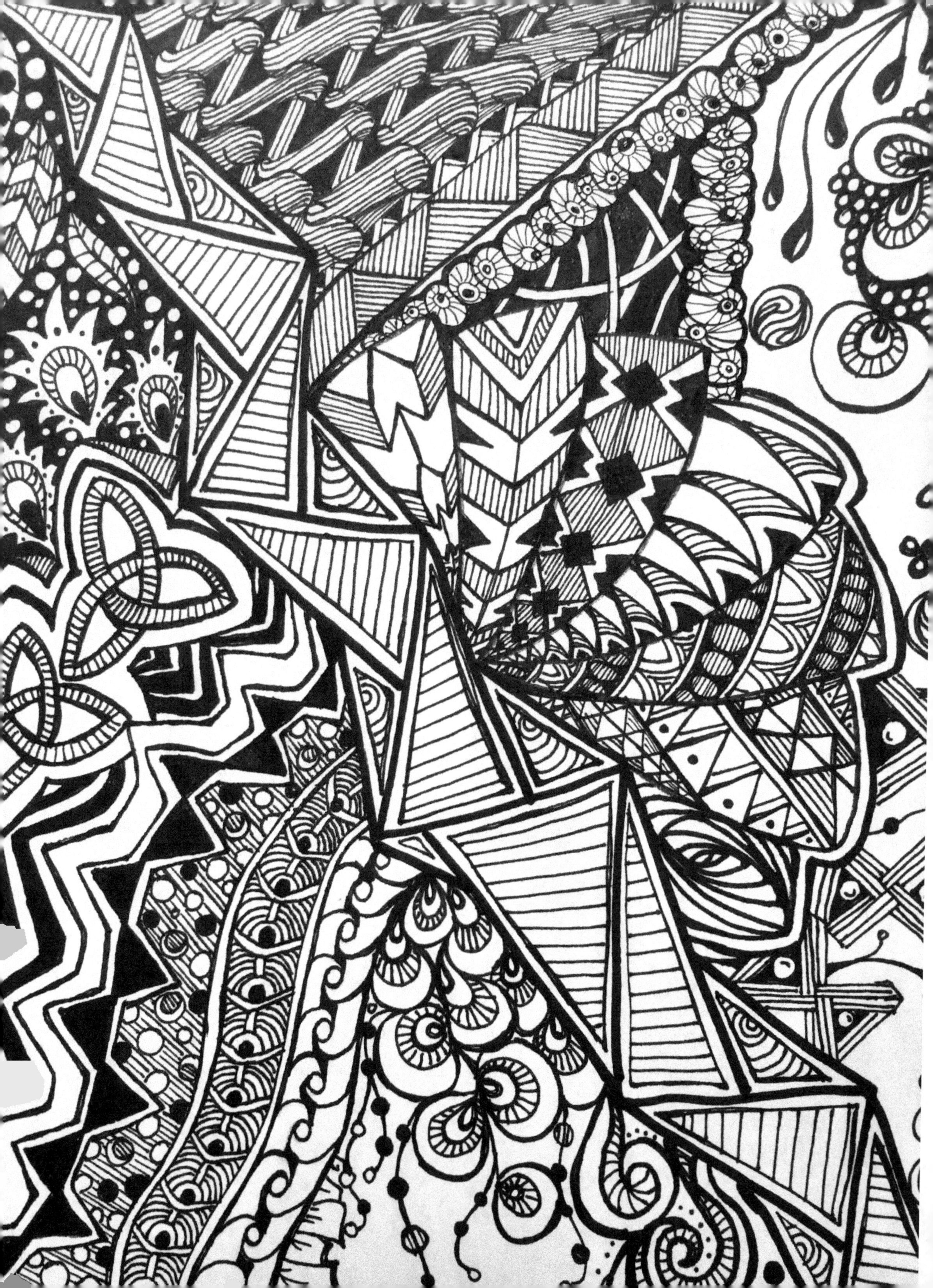

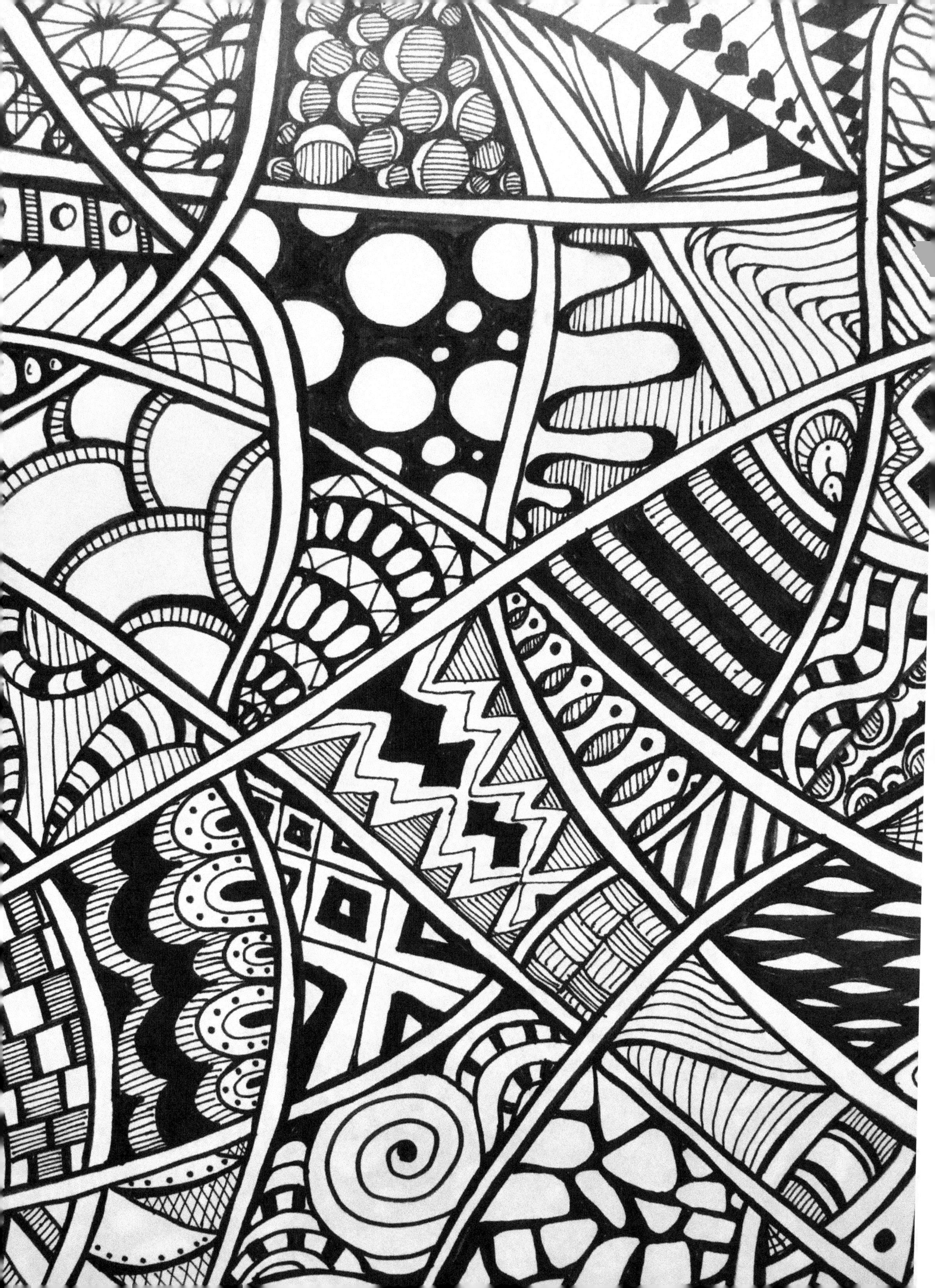

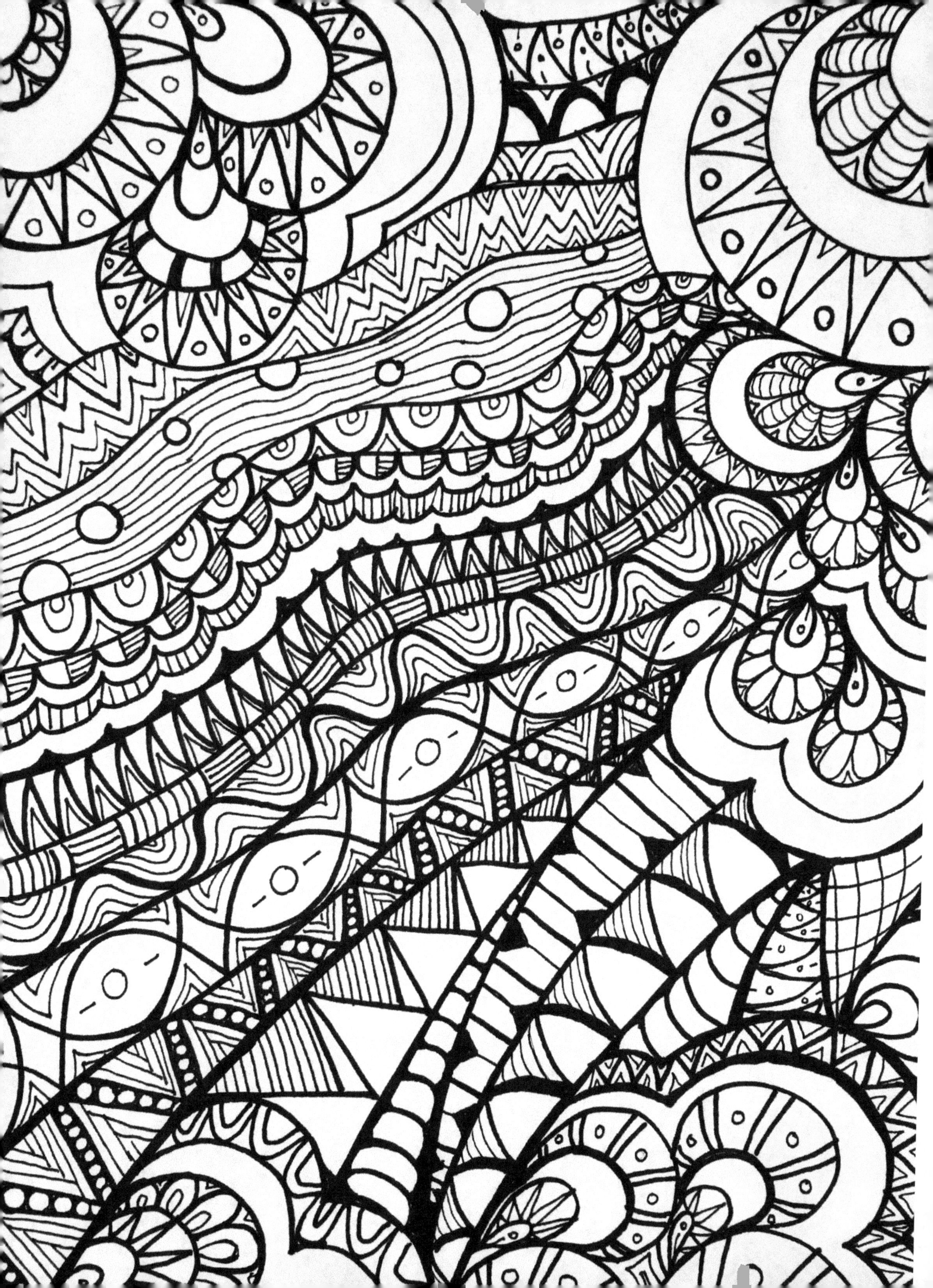

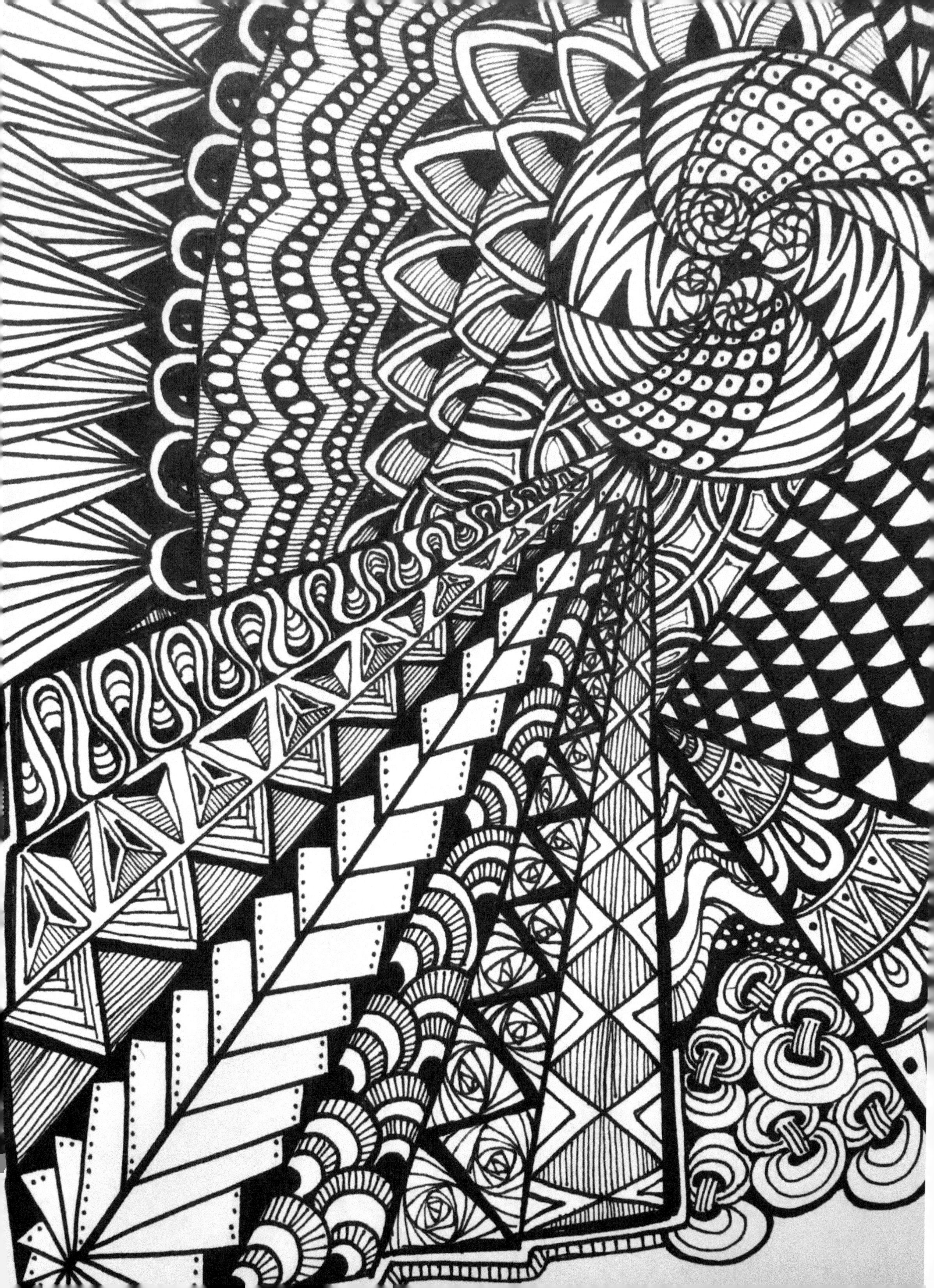

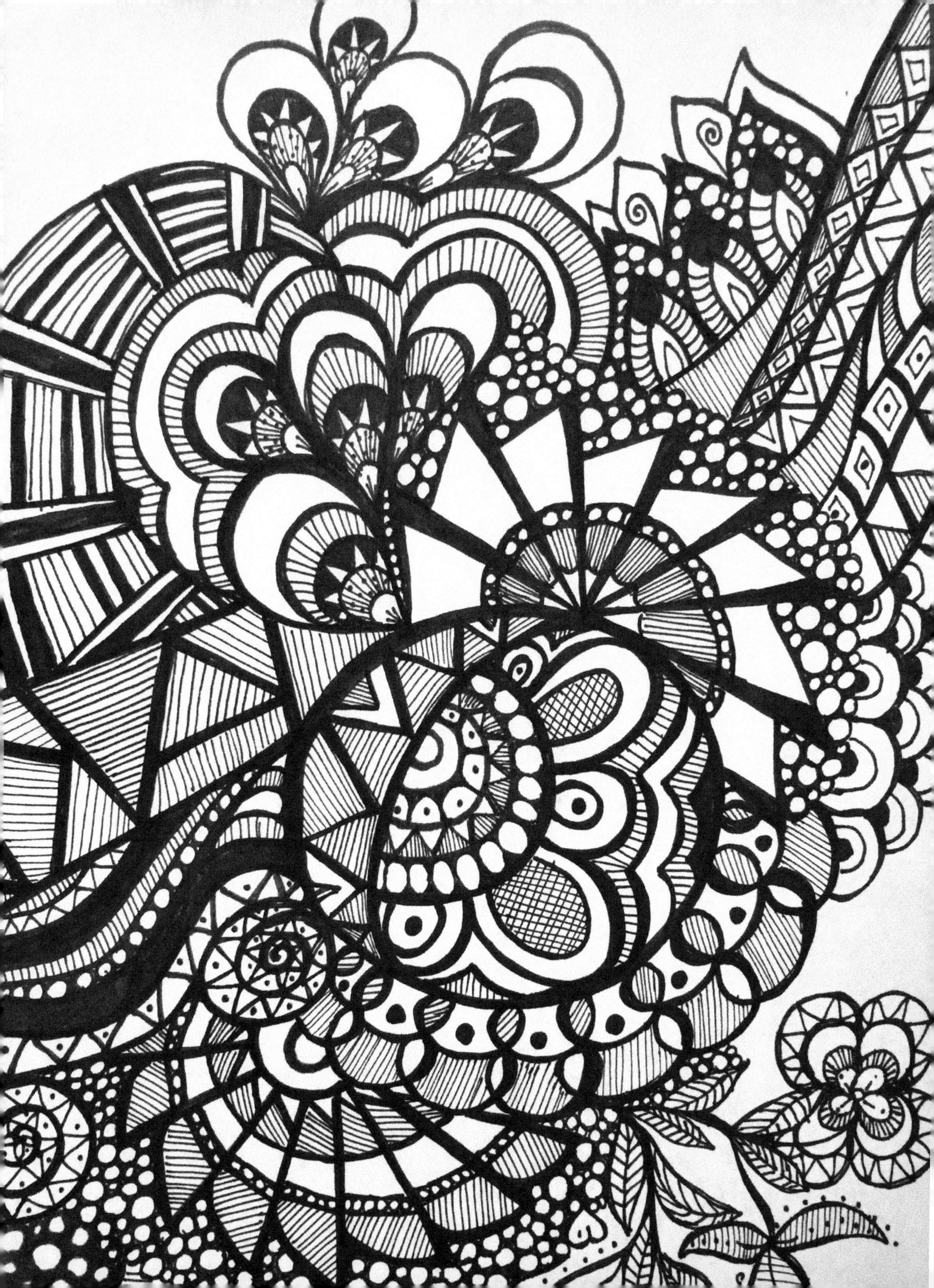

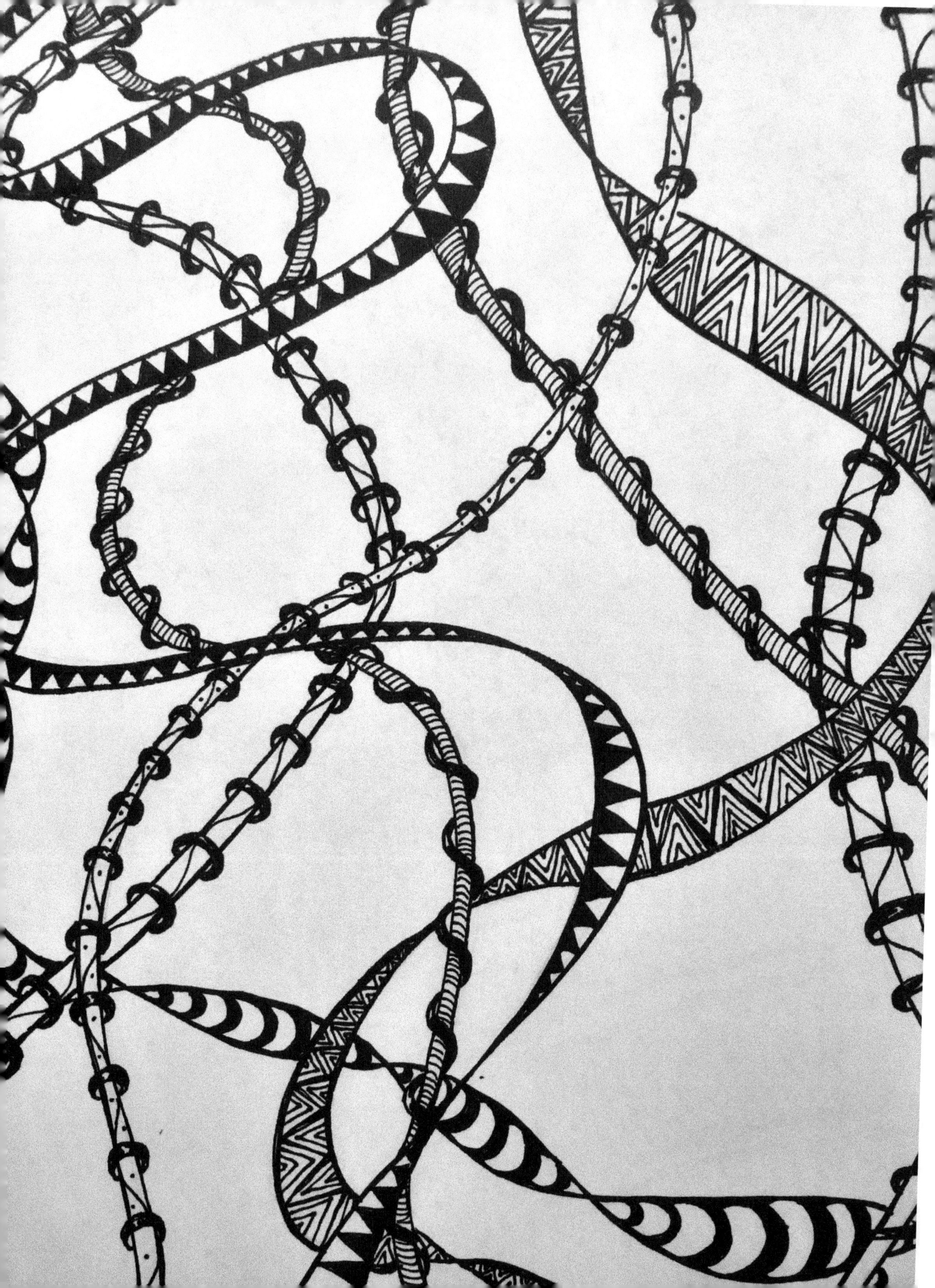

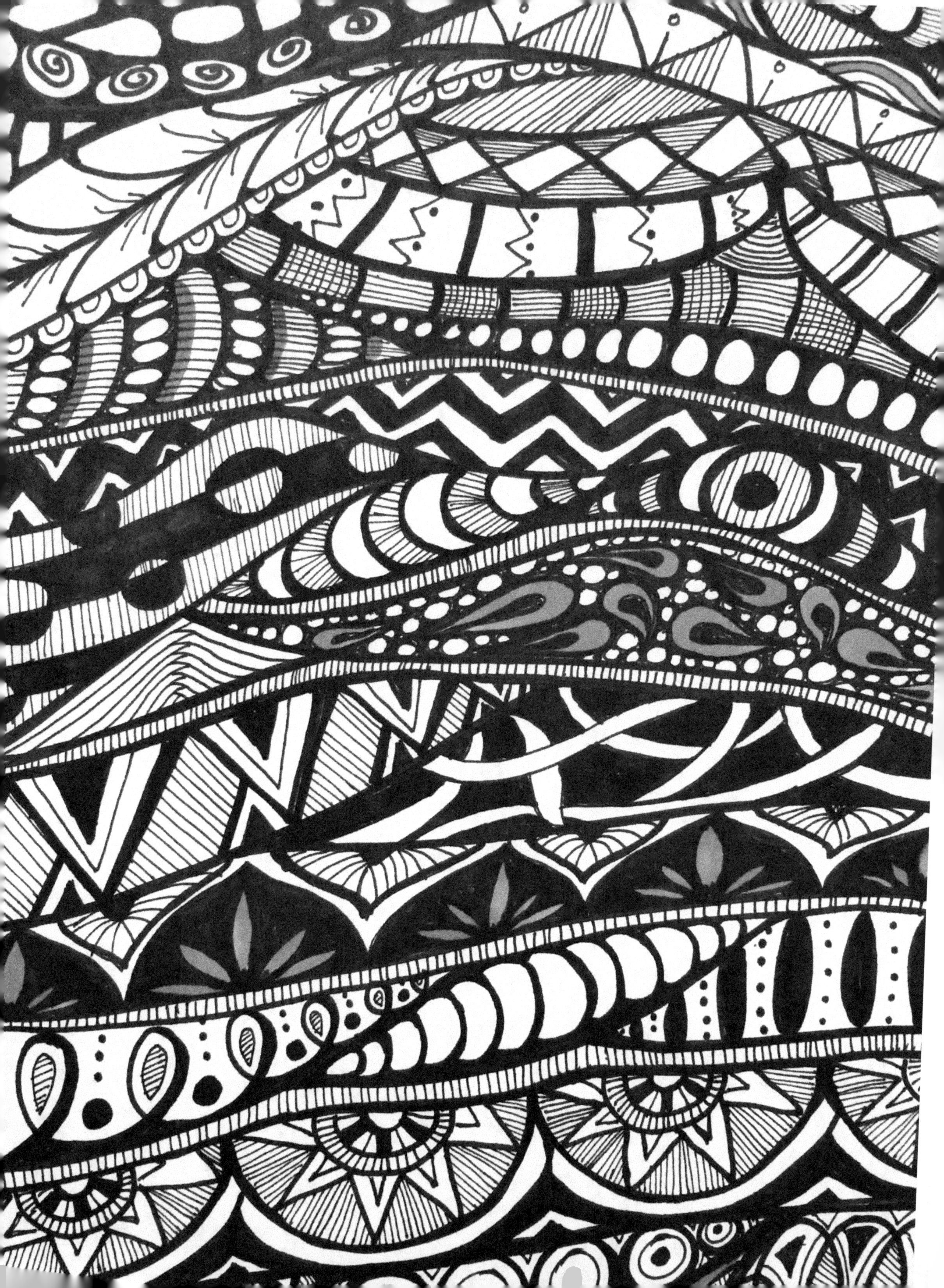

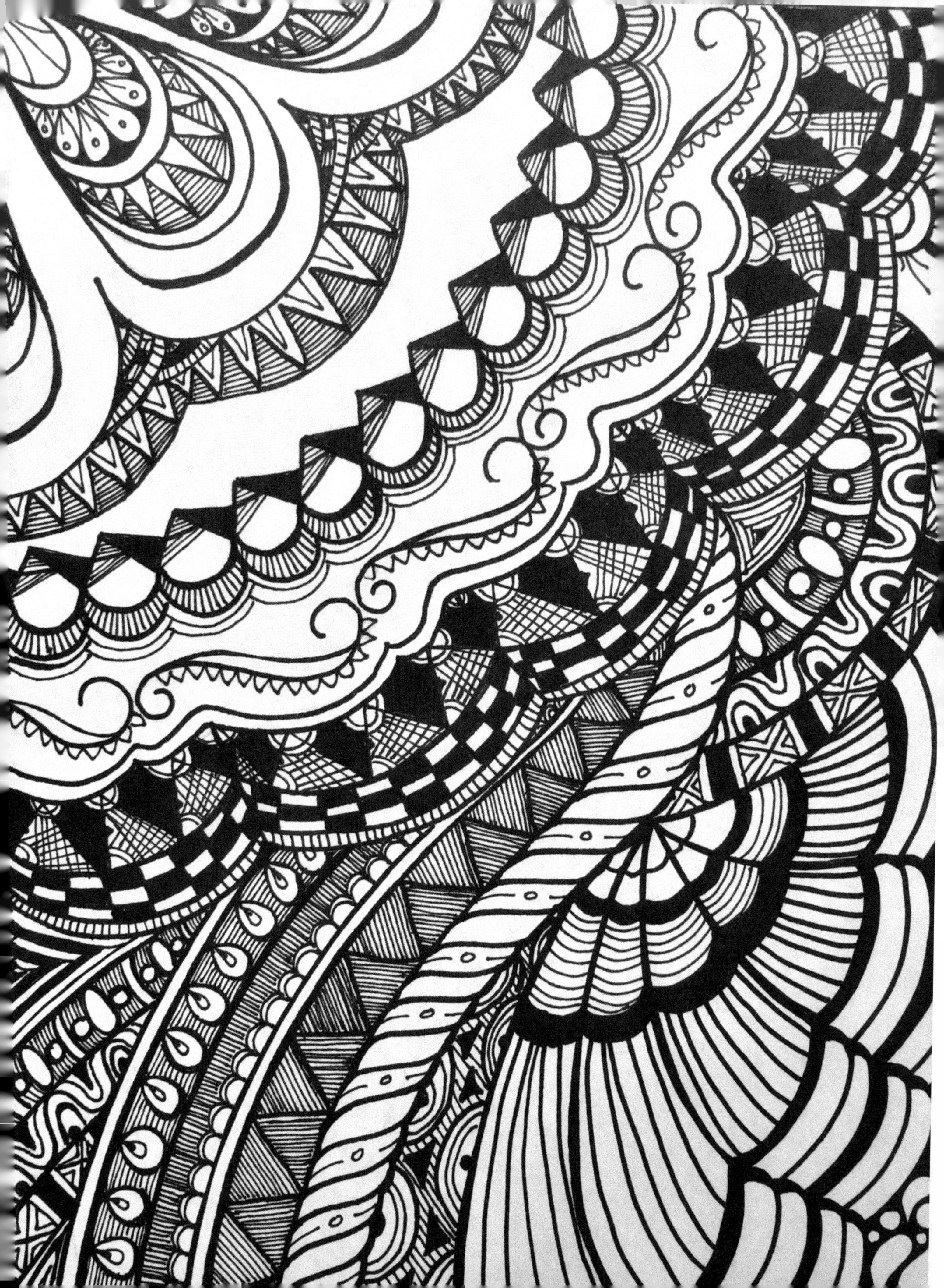

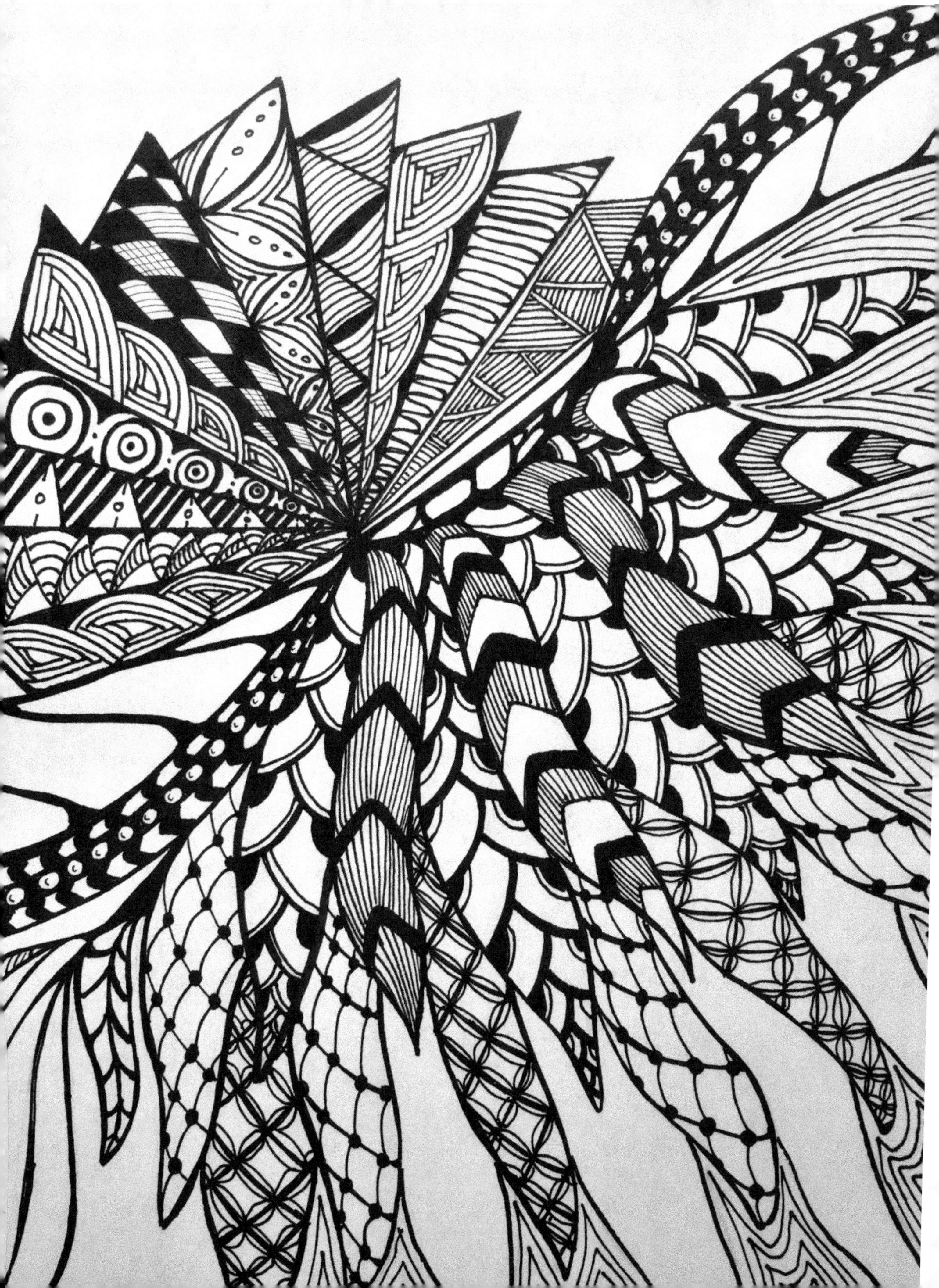

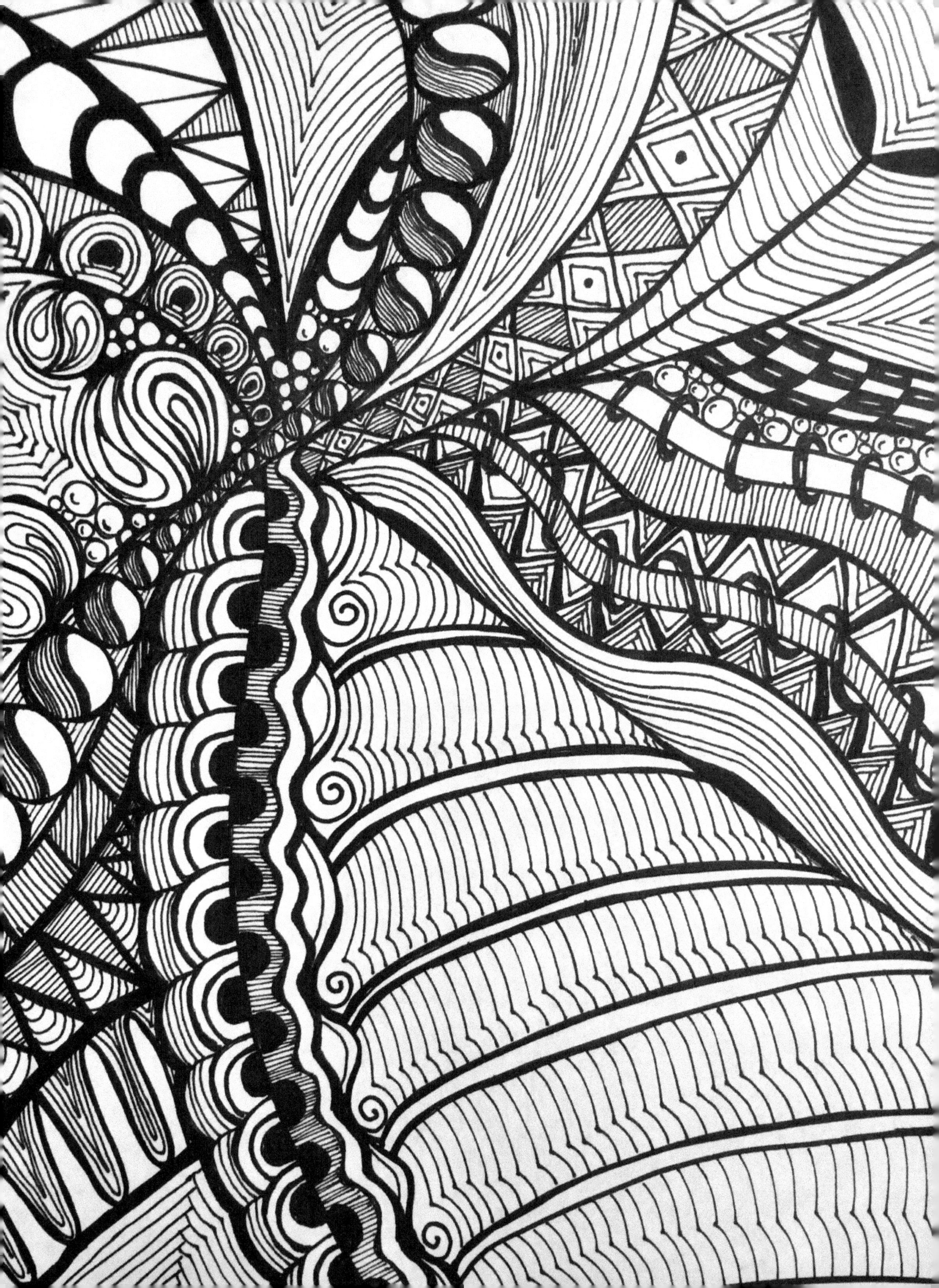

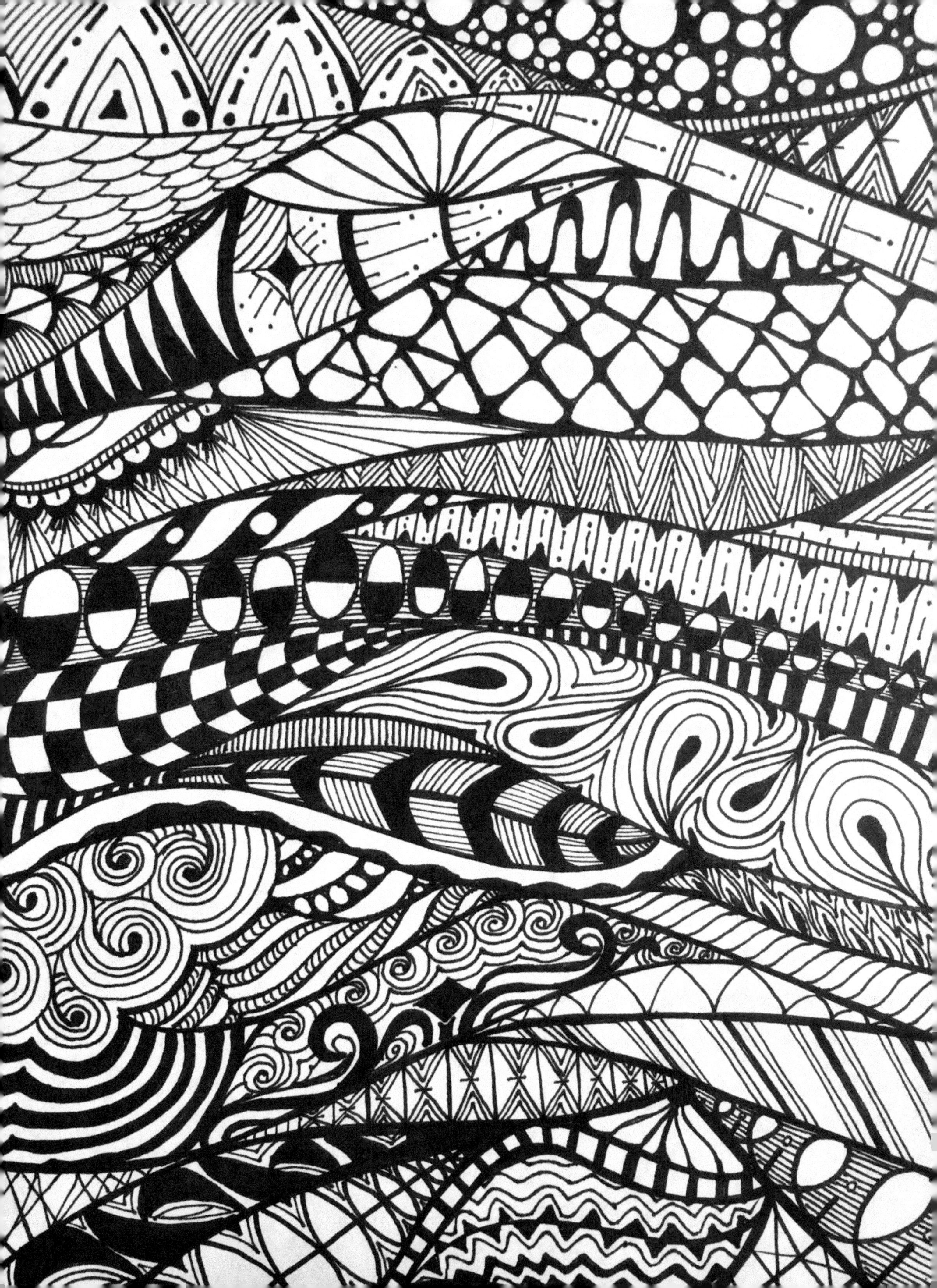

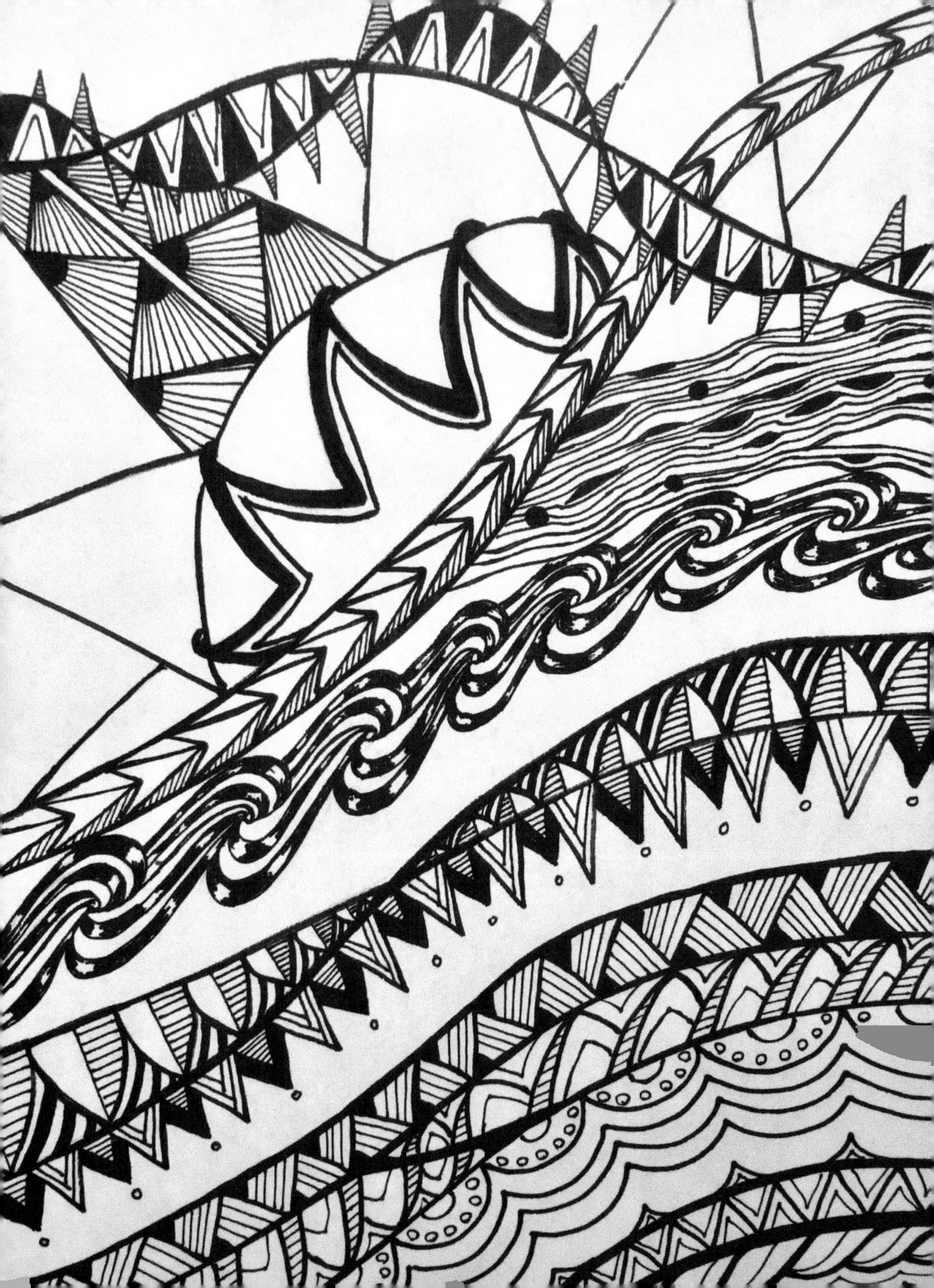

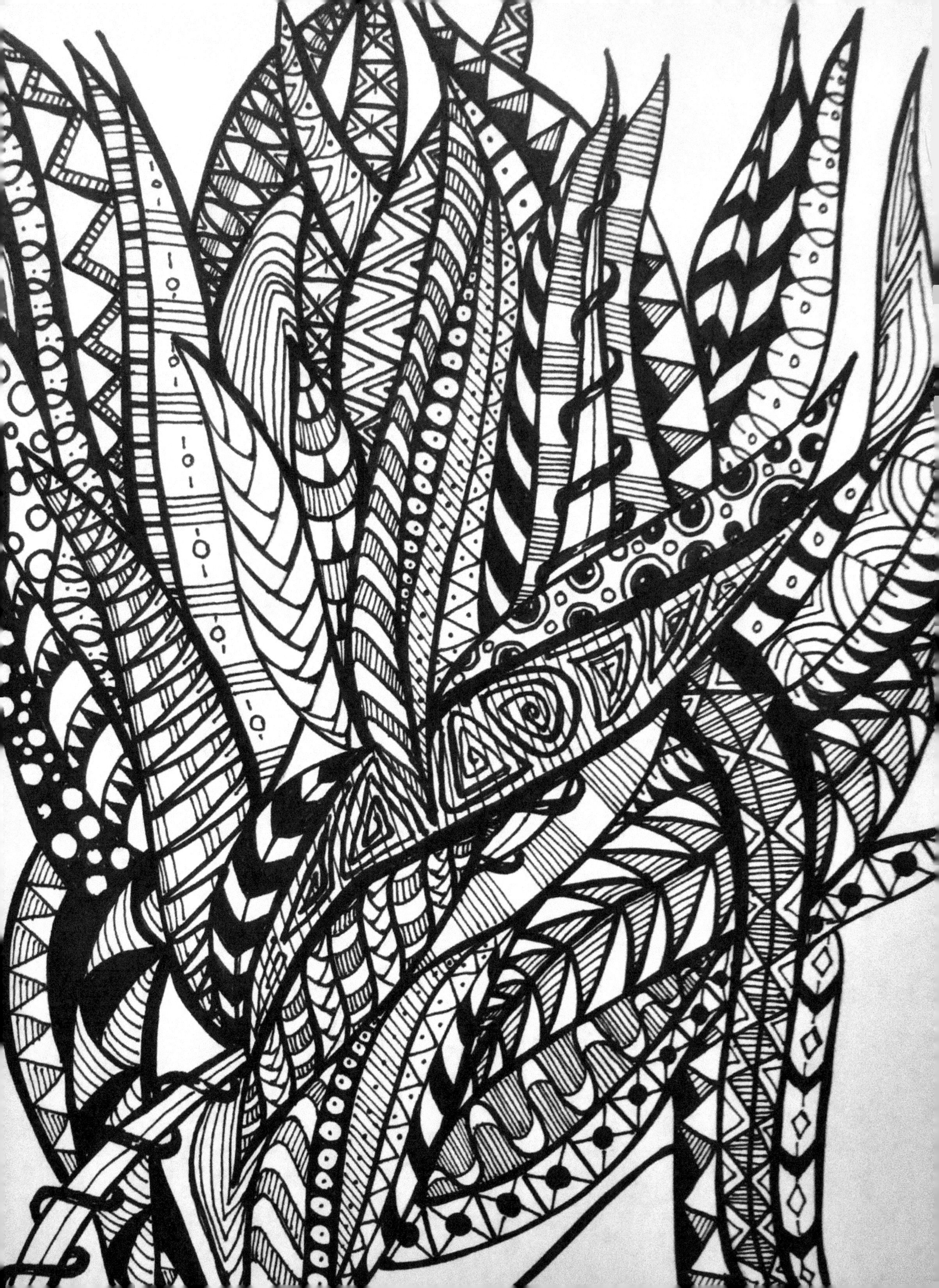

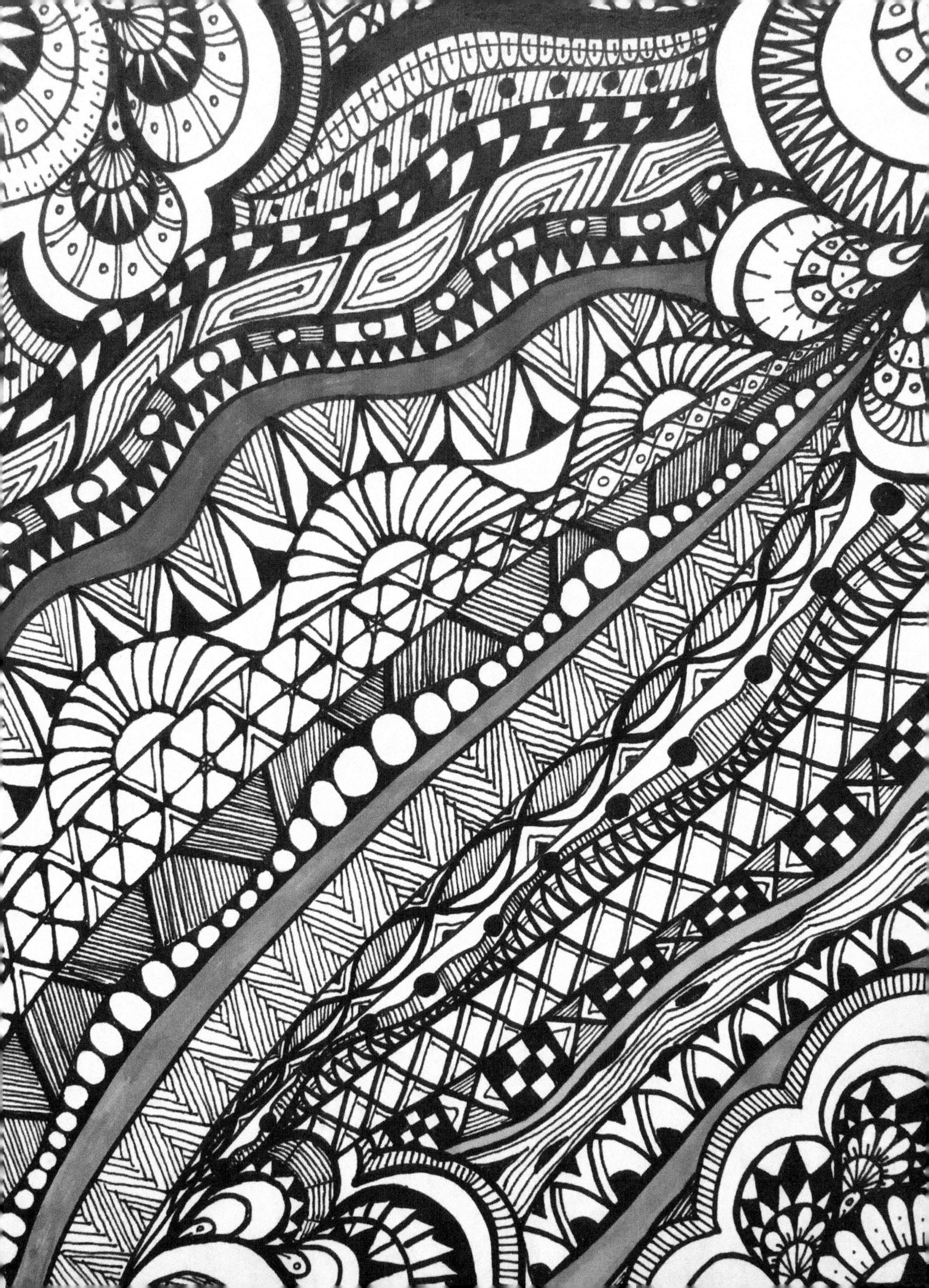

www.ingramcontent.com/pod-product-compliance
Lightning Source LLC
Chambersburg PA
CBHW060540210526
45170CB00019B/2501
* 9 7 8 1 5 4 6 9 9 7 7 1 9 *